APOSTROPHES
TO MYSELF

E. F. Dyck

Apostrophes to Myself

1987

oolichan books

Lantzville, British Columbia

Canadian Cataloguing in Publication Data

Dyck, E.F.
  Apostrophes to myself

  Poems.
  ISBN 0-88982-077-5

  I. Title.
  PS8557.Y24A74 1987   C811'.54   C87-091298-4
  PR9199.3.D92A74 1987

Publication of this book has been financially
assisted by the Canada Council.

Published by
OOLICHAN BOOKS
P.O. Box 10, Lantzville, B.C. V0R 2H0

Printed in Canada by
MORRISS PRINTING COMPANY LTD.
Victoria, British Columbia

For those
who gave me dolphins

Acknowledgements

Some of these poems have appeared in *CVII*, *Dandelion*, *Swift Current* (May 1987), and *Trace*, edited by Birk Sproxton (Winnipeg: Turnstone, 1986). The essay was published in *Grain* 14.2 (May 1986): 6-9. The author is grateful to their editors.

Contents

FOUND DOLPHINS

1

We saw dolphins in Mexico. When they came,
we went into the water to get a better view.
Their colour was black. They were very big.
We heard them breathing.

(Lara, 1979 AD)

2

It is the same with dolphins as with humans:
they come, side by side, male and female,
and mate; and the act extends over a time
which is neither very short nor very long.

(Aristotle, 4th Century BC)

TOPOGRAPHY

The land is wrinkled and folded like a brain.
It is grey in every season: grass of summer,
snow of winter, bare of spring and fall.
All these are grey and wrinkled and folded
as paper is folded in origami.

There are no rivers or lakes.
Long ago water covered everything:
now there are only eskers and
the tiled beds of dry lakes.

The waters have receded, the sea gone
underground, withdrawing through layers
and layers of grey soil growing whiter
and whiter till splash
         now the cool limpid sea
washes along the shores within.

The one sea is two seas that are one.
A corpus of land joins them, a bridge
between two waters.

ANATOMY I

You live within the sea
within your genital slit.

Your penis is your shape
exactly but red not grey.

You could hook a hawser
to it and tow a boat.

You erect and collapse it
at will (I envy you).

You make love to kelp
and caress mossy stones.

You know yourself, Dolphin,
you are phallus.

ANATOMY II

You live within the genital
slit within the sea.

You birth your own shape
exactly but white not grey.

You lift yourself out of the sea
into the quick element of heaven.

You swim with your image
nestled beside your flank.

You roll over to suckle
yourself from hidden breasts.

You nurture yourself, you
are womb, Dolphin.

I WANT YOU, HERMAPHRODITUS

There is no one to talk to but you,
Dolphin, oracle of the seas, no one.

No one understands the phallic thrust,
no one understands the spreading matrix,
no one understands the two in one.

When I speak from the corpus, the bridge
between two seas, I know that you hear me,
swimming, perhaps underneath me, flicking
your tail which thrusts you through the sea.

That is not enough:
my phallus wants your womb,
my womb wants your phallus.

But you never answer.

ARRESTED SPEED

I liked the gift you brought me:
she was young, her body was quick.

She was generous as well as prudent.
Arrested speed.

When you took the gift away I was
alone like you, caressing stones.

This is not a song of longing but of praise:
I praise the one path and the many;
I praise the black, the white, the grey;
I praise the meetings and the partings,

the dolphin on an anchor,
the outlaw held at bay.

YIN-YANG DOLPHIN

The Chinese lake-dolphin
is often mistaken for its opposite sex.
A legend tells us there is only one
such dolphin; another legend claims
there are three: a male, a female,
and the idea that there is only one.
A third legend says the lake-dolphin
is not a true dolphin.

Sometimes I thought I saw two of you
swimming round and round in a circle.

The surface of the lake was porcelain
waiting to be shattered when you jumped.

Once or twice I thought I saw a shadow
(or was it a flaw) in the opaque water.

I waited all day for the lake to crack,
I waited all day to be broken in two.

At sunset both of you broke free, rose up
arched, and slipped back under the water.

The lake did not break.
I did not shatter.

Male or female, subject or object, observer observed.
Behold the ancient tree, old puzzle, paradox of two!
This is the solution, the third.

MY DARK DARLING, MY DOLPHIN
(after a line by Nana Issaia)

Of smoked crystal, you flash in the half-light
of my bed, my dream, you my Tung Ting dolphin.

Your long nose is cruel and sharp, knifing
out of the bedsheets, jabbing the pillows.

Do you think you are playing in a mud-bed,
do you think I enjoy your mournful snuffles?

What sport! Breaching in a king-sized bed
where I like Moby Dick lie white, and dead!

I suppose I should feel joy, Dolphin,
I suppose play should engage the whale.

Against my white sheet you are a dark darling
of smoked crystal, a dear beast, a black light.

IN RELIEF

I saw his brown face and black hair,
I heard his voice soft from the past.

I looked into his black eyes and saw myself
as I once was, looking at his face, his eyes.

I was a seal in a zoo, snorting,
or a monkey, scratching my fleas.

The brown waters of the past pulled me
down, swept me along in a muddy river,

where, rolling in the current, you appeared,
Dolphin, brown god of the dark river gone,

a dolphin of Assyria, carved in relief
on a human form to counter human grief.

MORPHINE DOLPHIN

How is it possible that you swim inside your skin
unless you're drugged, stoned, doped to the eyeballs?

That is how you affect me, Dolphin, like morphine,
that third, that wakeful dream, that dreamed wake.

I become the precise opposite of ecstatic:
I go inside myself to the deep sea within.

You are supposed to swim faster than law allows,
I suppose I reach my destination before I begin.

As it is written, *In my end is my beginning*
as it is written, *In my beginning is my end.*

The first milky sea I swam in as a child
contained a tiny morphine dolphin, a hit

so imperceptible that I stagger, still.
Shall I ever wake to the real dream?

Shall I ever touch you without the dolphin
between, or swim like you without morphine?

THE DOLPHINS OF LUCRETIUS

Swerve from the straight and narrow fall
downward, into a limitless void, a deep.

By chance, deflect and bump.
Hook, coagulate, make lumps.

Parts of a whole, jostle a while
falling, copulating, falling.

Death is nothing to fear:
unhook, unzip, fall clear.

DOLPHIN OF DOLPHIN

If you were an eel, tail caught in mouth,
I'd understand (alpha and omega etcetera).

But you're a dolphin. What are you doing
swimming (asleep) in a vicious circle?

I suppose you suppose a dolphin
when you think *delphinus delphis*,

that your great whistling brain aches
when you escape by sounding the bottom

only to find yourself already losing
ballast, rising to meet yourself diving,

your self-reflection echoing wickedly
of yourself (Hi—haven't we met before?).

Everything here the shape of sound.
Far down is way up. This not a *koan*,

you idiot, this is how it all began,
this is how it ends: dolphin of dolphin.

BLUE DOLPHIN

Blue, how much I want you blue.
Blue wind, blue waves.

Blue dolphin, swimming gently on a tide,
shadow of a hull of a ship upon a sea.

This ship is not the memory of my desire,
this dolphin is not the desire of memory.

This ship is an old red car,
this dolphin is a bit of blue

plastic pinned to a grey roof,
this loss again is a gain.

DEFINITION OF DOLPHIN

They say you are the great precursor
of many families of lesser dolphins.

I will rescue you from that topos: *man fetches*
dolphin from place, from definition, from category!

A newer version of an old, old song—I replace
Arion and Dionysus, the child, the drunken fool.

Dolphinshit. (They play with their feces, you know,
not caring where they came from or how they sound.)

We speak of α-dolphins, β-dolphins, γ-dolphins,
talk of essence and accident, genus and species.

We know nothing: where do you come from, what
do you do, why did you do it, when and did you?

You are the cause of all causes
whose effects are themselves.

How you hurt me with joy when you breach!
Pain is a dolphin whose name is ecstasy.

How you never cry, never laugh,
always smile! We know nothing.

RICERCAR (OR, TO SEEK)

I have sought you, Dolphin,
and I have found you not.

According to your royal command.
Your canticle of canticles remains

upon division of division by two
a canon of canons encoding itself.

Your art is the art that delays,
your art is the art that defies.

To seek and not to find is
to seek to seek a dolphin.

HOW SHALL I SAY *HILLS*?

I went to catch a trout and hooked
a true hump-backed prairie dolphin.

Before my trout-fly landed,
a dolphin laughing took it

from the air and ran my line
from its reel and broke my rod

from my hand, and I lifted up my eyes
to the hills—how shall I say it truly?

A thousand dolphins rolled around me.
Their whistles made a western wind

that pressed the sagebrush into the cactus
and whipped the willows into crashing waves.

A thousand dolphins rose like hills up
to the sky, backs gleaming in the sun.

A thousand dolphins
at Fairwell Creek!

HE WORKS ON HIS TAN

Dozens of dolphins are lolling on the green,
turning and browning quite nicely thank you.

Their dark oiled bodies glisten in the sun.
Swimming school is over, holiday's begun.

It is time for him to get to work on his tan.
His belly will not do, it's as white as a fish's

and a bit flabby too, though a lovely lady once
remarked about *that certain attractive heaviness*

found only in the older dolphin
(as she frolic'd with a mindless youngster).

He knows he knows he knows:
the body grows thick, the mind thin,

in a punk world's din
the ear turns to tin,

words that mean and more
than three chords are sin.

He longs for the comfort of canon,
for the arrow that turns on itself.

Three blind dolphins, three blind dolphins,
see how they tan, see how they tan.
They tan all day in the burning sun,
it turns their bellies brown as buns.

So he works on his own tan, turning
belly-up, turning on himself, turning.

HE PLAYS A CLARINET

For him it was a natural mistake.
What he saw was what he heard and v.v.

He saw a lovely dolphinet
dark and subtle as a clarinet,

her siren shape of wood and slender
as a circle of arpeggios around a rock.

She was really just a common thing,
a bottle-nose, a B-flat clarinet

with sixteen keys and seven stops
her embouchure was only typical.

And yes, she clicked and squeaked
the light fantastic as he played.

But when he tried to make her scale
she honked. She simply wouldn't bottle-

nose for him: no mellow liquid trills,
no breathy low notes, no plummets.

The dolphin played the dolphinet
as best he could—but it was bad.

To make me register, she said at last,
you have to use your thumb!

The dolphin is a moody fellow, and at once
he drifted slowly downward like a helix,

thumbing his nose as he sank,
thumbing his nose as he fell.

For him it was a natural mistake,
for what he heard was what he saw:

and he heard a subtle clarinet
as dark and lovely as a dolphinet.

A THEORY OF COMMUNICATION

The channel-dolphin swims back and forth,
a noisy creature, full of snorts and clicks.

At one end of the channel, he appears uncertain:
what to do what to do what to do what a to do.

When he makes up his mind, he turns like a swimmer
and zips up-channel, butterflying like crazy.

He plays with the message as he moves along:
he runs it forwards, he runs it backwards,

he invents more efficient codes—most of all,
he increases his load of entropy.

This tires him out and he slows down. Sometimes
he even stops to rest. Once, he turned back

and floated all day in mid-channel. At the far end
there was panic—the decoding manuals said nothing

about what to do when the message didn't arrive.
The chief decoder, snorting and clicking,

had to be restrained from jumping into the channel
with snorkel and fin to search for the message.

Meanwhile, the dolphin had found a dolphinet,
they were happily nosing and biting each other.

They were making love silently,
the message all medium.

AN ALTERNATE THEORY

On the other flipper,
sometimes the dolphin is very sure.

A is A, he squeaks, *and B B, C C*,
as he thrusts his nose into a ring.

And "if A," he continues, *"Then B"*—
or is it "if B then A?"   Doubt,

the echo of an echo, rises with a bump
and exponentially subsides to nothing.

A or not-A, he sings, but his nose feels
constricted, his song sounds a bit flat.

A or not-A, he recourses, more unsure
of his sureness, swimming now in circles,

the band of truth on his bottle-nose
tightening as a love-ring on a swelling.

Information information zero infinity
he can't decide if he can decide if

he is being led around by the nose
or is he nosing around by the truth?

His nose hurts, the ring is tight,
he gulps for air as best he can and dives.

He dives until the singing in his head
rises to the shriek of *danger danger*

this is the deep unknowable deep
fathoms flashing past and cold

the unknown pressing in upon him
from the outside shrinks his nose

and the ring of truth
slips off and sinks

a tiny golden sound
lost forever in the dark.

He releases all his air in a rush
and rolls over and over and deeper.

It is quiet here in his head.
Only the switch of yesno gates.

Only endorphins
can save him now.

PHAETON AND APOLLO AND THE DOLPHINS

They no longer play on the surface.
I lost control, drove my chariot

which was really a red flasher of a car,
running wild, burning, the world on fire.

The great prairie turned into a desert:
its people burned, they turned black.

I should have listened to my father:
I am old, he said, *where have they gone?*

They have gone underground, the surface
is hot, the deep is cool, the heat burns

their lungs when they come up for air
they no longer play on the surface.

WINTER

On a clear winter day the sun
glows red as the harvest moon.

Dolpins flicker on the white
water—they of course can see

nothing, naturally blind to the light
their eyes loll in their sockets white.

The dolphins are not feeding. Under the unseen
red sun they are swimming away from themselves.

Great strips of skin peel from their backs.
The flesh beneath is the colour of their eyes.

The dolphins, white on the white water,
invisible under the red burning sun.

They cannot see, they could never see.
They cannot be seen as once they were.

Once, they spoke with each other,
they heard the other's cry, answered.

Now they make no sounds that they hear,
though they breathe and whistle and click.

They sing—but they cannot hear where
they are, they cannot see where there

is no ear to see, where there is only one
dolphin alone among a thousand other dolphins

singing a song that he himself cannot hear,
this cry from his heart, this song of winter.

It is winter. Spring is winter. Summer
is winter. Fall is winter.

Winter, under the red
dying sun.

GOODBYE DOLPHINS
(for Gloria)

It was your courage
which surprised me most
that day on the Punta Banda.
And we did see the dolphins again,
as though answering what you had scratched
on the sand with a stick. *Goodbye dolphins*
you had written on the sand like a child,
will we see you again?

Why do I weep now remembering the past?
That brave thing you did with stick and sand
makes me want to pass through your eye like light
makes me want to take that woman by her hand
makes me want to hold that child fast.

The dolphins swim, still, along the Punta Banda
where we played with kelp-snakes washed ashore
where we built nightfires in a ring of tin.
But I am torn and tormented,
memories measure my fears.

Will we see them again?
Will we be brave?

AFTERWORD

The Rhetoric of Language (or, the Choice)

Perhaps it is surprising that contemporary restatements of the nature of language originate with Nietzsche. Usually associated with notions of Superman or with cults of the binary—Dionysus versus Apollo—Nietzsche pointed out that language is in its essential nature rhetorical; language is always *doxa* (opinion) rather than *episteme* (knowledge); words are always, technically speaking, tropical (even simple statements like "the tree is green" are either metaphorical or metonymical); and the history of language usage attests to the centrality of the rhetorical triad, ethos/logos/pathos (or, the writer-speaker/the written-spoken/the reader-listener) ("Lecture Notes on Rhetoric," 1874). In other words, Nietzsche's argument is that rhetoric is not something added to language but something intrinsic to language. As many writers have discovered, the choice is not whether to use rhetoric. . . .

Contemporary treatments of language shun the word (but not the concept) of rhetoric. Northrop Frye, for example, identifies rhetoric and oratory, or public speaking, and uses the word only in his discussion of the first phase (hieroglyphic-metaphoric) of language development (*The Great Code*, 1982). But his treatment of this and the later phases (hieratic-metonymic, demotic-descriptive) is quite obviously infused with rhetorical considerations as even the choice of labels shows. Indeed, if anything characterizes contemporary discussions of language (and of writing), it is their universal "terror of [the word] rhetoric" (Genette's phrase). Structuralism admits it has its "august forbearer, . . . rhetoric" (Jonathan Culler, *Structuralist Poetics*, 1975); deconstructionism's pre-occupation with the presence/absence of the speaker and with a demonstration of aporia (say, of matter versus manner) is a rhetorical pre-occupation (Jacques Derrida, *Of Grammatology*, 1974); and an emergent feminist or womanist approach to language alerts us to the hidden forces (a favourite 19th century rhetorical term) of language's "amniotics" (I use this word rather than Kristeva's (ab)use of the word "semiotics" to describe non-symbolic language functions; *Desire for Language*, 1980). Eagleton's views on "literature" and "criticism" reveal their inherent ideologies and advocate a re-invention of rhetoric for our time (*Literary Theory*, 1983); and Easthope's *Poetry as Discourse* (1984) unwittingly suggests, in a truncated fashion, how such a re-invention might take place. Language, whether considered in the large or in the small, seems to presuppose rhetoric. Once again, the choice is not whether to use rhetoric. . . .

A rhetorical conception of language is however rather unflattering to received notions of self, of meaning, of truth. It says flatly that language is dirty; the motives of the language-user are always implicated; reference is always ambiguous; truth is never finally won. Falstaff says, "What is honor? A word" (*1 Henry IV*); Eliot despairs, "Words strain, Crack and sometimes break under the burden" ("Burnt Norton"). On the other hand, a rhetorical conception of language encourages play and re-creation. It says that fiction (like history) is a "false document" of a truth (Doctorow), that poetry is "the strange rhetoric" of the relations between mind and matter (Stevens), that language is our mother (Marlatt) and our father (Lacan). William Gass's long philosophical poem *On Being Blue*

(1976) and Anne Szumigalski's ruminations on the nature of motorcycling and poetics (*Risks*, 1983) are rhetorical treatises of serious playfulness. Eco's *The Name of the Rose* (1980), which recreates the lost part of Aristotle's poetics, and Geoffrey Ursell's *Perdue* (1984), which recreates the loss of the West, are serious plays on the same *topos*, that place called "what-if." The vision underlying disparate authors and works, in several continents and many eras, is remarkable in its uniquely rhetorical nature—and the temptation to multiply Canadian examples is almost irresistible (Wah, Lane, Page, Atwood, . . .). We are, it seems, a dialectic, and our choice is not whether to use rhetoric. . . .

Perhaps it is equally surprising that the restatements of the nature of language that begin with Nietzsche actually continue a tradition that dates to Aristotle. It is a hopeless task to consider that tradition in an essay such as this; it is hopeless even to consider one aspect of that tradition. What I offer instead is an inadequate trace of one such aspect, a small part of the story of language-as-rhetoric, the story, in outline, of the literary symbol.

Prairie writing, as we are all aware, is full of crows (though Paul Hiebert argues strongly for the snearth). And the crow, as we all know, is no Phoenix, ending its life not in perfumes but in the rag-and-bone-shop of the carrion heart. So how is it that the crow in prairie literature reproduces and regenerates itself without (apparently) any outside help? For we know what the crow is: "any one of those several oscine birds of the genus *Corvus*, of the family *Corvidae*, having lustrous black plumage, as the common crow, *brachyrhyncos*, of North America." An even earlier question: how did the word *crow* and the thing *crow* get together? Plato's Cratylus would have us believe that the

43

two are "naturally" fitted—but any prairie boy knows that roosters crow whereas crows don't. Aristotle went a step further: the written word *crow*, he would have said, is a symbol of the spoken word *krō*, which in turn is a symbol of the mental experience of crow. And so began semiotics, the science of relegating written language to a copy of a copy (spoken language) of the real thing (it's all in the head, you know). As if that wasn't complicated enough, Aristotle went on: the word *crow*, he would have said, will be applied to things that it doesn't apply to—and how right he was (overlooking, of course, that perhaps *crow* doesn't really apply to crows, either). As I said, roosters crow, hence, metaphor (too bad he wasn't a ten) hiding itself in the possibilities of language.When Lorna Uher wrote *Crow's Black Joy* (1978), that was a metaphor; when she recovered her name *Crozier*, it became synecdoche—part for whole or vice versa, species for genus or vice versa, a trick built into language that makes us "realize many meanings in one" (Quintilian, *Institutio Oratoria*).

I myself am fond of dolphins. Many years ago I heard the inimitable Allan McFee refer on his radio show to a pod of white whales swimming under the prairie near Edmonton. St. Augustine would have said he was using conventional signs at a figurative level (*On Christian Doctrine*), and he might have speculated that McFee spoke of *white* whales because he was delivering a coded message to those worthy of decoding it. Anyway, those white whales became my grey dolphins which (like, I suspect, McFee's whales) were not tied or hobbled to any code that I could name. Quite simply, the dolphins swam in my mind. Being a realist, I went to Mexico with Gloria and Lara in the summer of 1979 to observe the dolphins in their natural habitat. The dolphin, I was convinced, was not a metaphor, was rather a part of something it represented, and to find out what that something could be, I had to see some action. The Renaissance rhetoricians would have said I was using a trope based on division rather than on comparison (Dudley Fenner, *The Artes of Loglike and Rhetorike*, 1584).

For quite some time I made no progress, linear or otherwise. My imagination was fired, it is true, by what we saw in Mexico. The sight of a prairie dolphin, breaching on the far side of a bay off the interior coast of the Baja, stunned me. There he was, going up, "out of his element," hanging fire for a moment in the air lit by the setting sun, and then he was down and gone. A shout along the beach where we were camping: "Dolphins! They're jumping!" That it was in Spanish simply did not matter, and the next morning Lara soberly recorded in her nine-year-old's journal what we had seen and done when we rose: "We went into the water to get a better view [of the dolphins]. Their colour was black, They were very big. We heard them breathing." I returned to Saskatchewan and read everything I could find about the prairie dolphin. What I learned can be briefly put: "... the Sign and its Explanation [of its relation to its Object] make up another sign, and since it will probably require an additional explanation... [etc.]... we shall or should ultimately reach a Sign of Itself, containing its own explanation and those of its significant parts, and according to this explanation each part has some other part as its object" (C. S. Peirce, 1910). Yes, I said to myself, *that* is the dolphin. "It... partakes of the reality which it renders intelligible; and while it enunciates the whole, abides itself as a living part in that Unity, of which it is the representative" (Coleridge, *Biographia Literaria*, 1817).

Rhetoric did not of course discover the dolphin (there it was, swimming under the prairie, inside my head); nor could rhetoric determine what the dolphin referred to, signified, or meant; in short, rhetoric could not establish *why* or to *what* the dolphin persuaded. But the dolphin was persuasive, it was itself, it was part of something else. What rhetoric could do was to alert me to the means of persuasion in this instance—it could, in other words, suggest *how*. I would write the persuasion of the dolphin into being— *Logos* as word, speech, account, argument. Ah, but who was "I"? *Ethos*—narrator, speaker, character—this persuader, too, I would create in my text. And who would be persuaded by this? *Pathos* traditionally evokes the experience of events by an audience; my audience became the dolphin whom I addressed, who was swimming about in my head, that is myself. That is, synecdoche.

—from *Grain* Volume XIV, Number 2 (May 1986):6-9.

E. F. Dyck was born in Turnhill, Saskat-
chewan in 1939. He attended the University
of Saskatchewan, the University of Minne-
sota, and the University of Manitoba. He
has taught Mathematics and English at the
university level. His previous books of poems
include *Odpoems &* (1978), *The Mossbank
Canon* (1982), and *Pisscat Songs* (1983).